CONTENTS

PREFACE

THE three sonatas written by Beethoven in 1783, when he was thirteen years old, were published with a statement by his father that they were written at the age of eleven; but unfortunately his father was not consistent in his methods of advertising the infant prodigy. Sometimes he post-dated the child's birth and sometimes he ante-dated the works. To us these early sonatas are remarkable enough as the work of a child of thirteen. Still, a good deal of growth can be accomplished between the ages of eleven and thirteen; and in 1783 Mozart had only just produced *Die Entführung aus dem Serail*, and did not write *Le nozze di Figaro* until three years later. The example of his amazing childhood was in all men's minds, wherever his name was mentioned; and Johann van Beethoven was bent on making a similar sensation with his son. He overworked the child with practice on the violin, in addition to his very thorough studies of the pianoforte, the organ and composition. Perhaps a trace of the child's efforts on the violin may be found in the curious and unpractical imitations of minute violin-bowings with which Beethoven's juvenile pianoforte works are covered. On the other hand, such fussy detail is natural enough in a child who is capable of such advanced work as these very presentable little sonatas. It is doubtful whether he could himself break up his semiquavers on the pianoforte in that fashion. An attempt to do so would have reduced his *allegros* to *andantes;* and there are other juvenile qualities in these compositions which would be more likely to lead him to play too fast than too slow. Young players cannot too soon learn to respect the tiniest details of the works of even the youngest masters.

Johann van Beethoven was a poor drink-sodden creature whose growing incapacity left Ludwig virtually head of the family before he was fifteen. But it would be a mistake to see nothing but squalor in Beethoven's early life. Except, perhaps, as regards the violin, none of the child's early accomplishments were forced upon him. At a time when J. S. Bach was regarded merely as the scholastic father of several more accomplished sons, the boy Beethoven could play the whole of *Das Wohltemperierte Clavier* by heart. This was no fashionable accomplishment for an infant prodigy, and can no more have been forced upon him than it was forced upon the boy Walter Parratt some seventy years later. The Beethoven family was practically in the domestic service of the Archbishop-Elector of Cologne, whose palace is now the University of Bonn. Cultivated people such as the Breunings took pains to see that the boy should come into contact with an intellectual civilisation worthy of his gifts. Certainly there is nothing provincial about these early sonatas. Bonn was a good musical centre, and musical historians find much to interest them in the works of the musicians, such as Dal'Abaco, who settled there before

Beethoven was born. But the young Beethoven shows more clearly the influence of composers he knew only by reputation, or who visited Bonn only in passing. Carl Philipp Emmanuel Bach was still composing in 1783; and to the young Beethoven his style was the perfection of romance. (Incidentally, we may observe that a revival of C. P. E. Bach, in an edition adapted for the use of young players, is long overdue.)

The most remarkable thing about these juvenile sonatas is not their style, but their form. It is by no means infallible; there are whole movements, such as the Presto of the F minor Sonata, where the composer indicates *presto* in vain, as the pace can make no headway against the uniform length of its phrases. No wonder that in such a movement the child gets tired and, like Haydn at the age of twenty-three, writes a perfunctory second part. But elsewhere the miscalculations are signs of promise, for they concern intentional contrasts of length such as do not enter into the calculations of commonplace composers at all. Thus, in the first movement of the D major Sonata, towards the end of the exposition, there are three big chords and a dramatic pause followed by a cadence-group. The dramatic gesture does not quite come off, and the cadence-group is not quite convincingly balanced. But the child knows what he meant; and students have often done advanced compositions without expressing anything so clearly. Again, in the same movement, bars 22 to 29 seem dangerously broad. But it is not by inadvertence that in bars 80 to 85 the child has recapitulated them in three-bar rhythm instead of four-bar rhythm.

It is curious to find Master Ludwig least successful in handling the Rondo form. In the Rondo of the E flat Sonata there seems to be one episode too many, and the end is unconvincing. For the rest, the form of these sonatas is highly creditable to everyone concerned; and surely a good word is due to the Court Organist Neefe, under whose auspices these juvenile works were published. The ornaments as printed consist almost exclusively of the sign for the Pralltriller,

applied often in the most unsuitable places. It is probable that it sometimes stands for the true mordent

and sometimes for the turn, . All ordinary shakes will have turns at the end. Young Beethoven, as a devout lover of C. P. E. Bach, would surely endorse that master's opinion that a shake without a turn is almost inconceivable.

The unfinished Sonata in C major is in quite a different category from the others. It cannot have been written long before the sonatas in Opus 2, and the first movement, for all its slenderness in dimensions and sound, is as masterly as anything in that Opus. The modulations in the development are particularly beautiful, and the recapitulation shows the highest mastery of form and tonality in the way in which it represents part of the second group in the sub-dominant, as a result of the unusually slight emphasis on the dominant key in the exposition. In bar 1, Beethoven gives minim heads to the first notes of the quaver groups; these may be taken to indicate a *legatissimo* touch in all these groups throughout the movement. The slow movement Beethoven left unfinished just as he had begun his recapitulation. His pupil, F. Ries, finished it from bar 26, and finished it correctly enough on recapitulatory lines until his last three bars, which are obviously almost nonsensical. I have, therefore, relegated those three bars to an appendix and finished the movement on what seems to me a more likely plan.

The authenticity of the two Sonatinas in G and F has been questioned. They are pleasing little studies in melodic form, and there is no reason why Beethoven should not have written them, though I have often doubts as to the coda of the Romance in the G major Sonatina. On the other hand, there is no reason why Beethoven should have written them; and they do not show the fussy imitation violin-phrasing of his juvenile works. Moreover, they were published after his death, when his name on the title page would guarantee their sale. But at least they deserve the benefit of the doubt.

DONALD FRANCIS TOVEY

Sonat(in)a in E flat

WoO 47/1

8

(a)

Andante

RONDO
Vivace

Sonat(in)a in F minor

WoO 47/2

Larghetto maestoso

Allegro assai

(a)

Sonat(in)a in D
WoO 47/3

MENUETTO
Sostenuto

VAR. I [l'istesso tempo]

VAR. IV

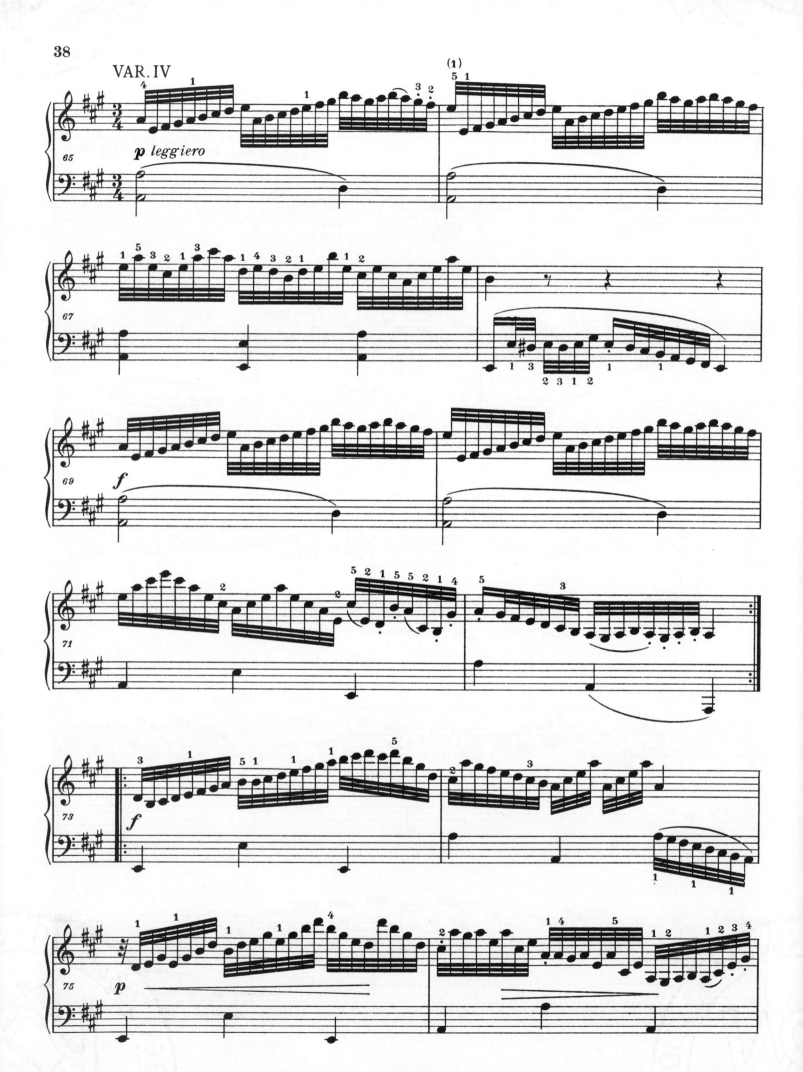

39

A.B.1840

VAR. VI.

SCHERZANDO
Allegro, ma non troppo

Sonat(in)a in C

WoO 51

Adagio

* From bar 26 the movement is finished by Beethoven's pupil F. Ries, whose reading is here adopted till bar 32, after which point it seems capable of improvement. Bars 33 to 38 are by D. F. Tovey.

Version of the ending
by F. Ries

Sonatina in G

Anh.5/1

Marks of nuance in this Sonatina are almost entirely editorial and have not been bracketed.

A.B.1840

ROMANZE
Allegretto espressivo

Sonatina in F
Anh. 5/2

RONDO
Allegro

Two movements of a Sonatina

WoO 50

Allegretto

3:04

Printed and bound in Great Britain by Caligraving Limited